CW01496426

A JOURNEY THROUGH LIFE

Though we tread our different paths in life, for all of us there are significant moments, perhaps arising from chance meetings or small incidents, when life takes on a new meaning. We gain new insights and perhaps we even glimpse what is to come.

At every stage, it is important to observe, learn and develop, and to be ready to see each day as a new beginning for a happier and brighter future.

In this selection of poetry by Jacqueline Lesley Davies Bell, the author shares the experiences and lessons of her own Journey Through Life.

A
JOURNEY
THROUGH LIFE

Jacqueline Lesley Davies Bell

ARTHUR H. STOCKWELL LTD
Torrs Park   Ilfracombe   Devon
Established 1898
www.ahstockwell.co.uk

British Library Cataloguing-in-Publication Data.
A catalogue record for this book is available
from the British Library.

ISBN 978-0-7223-3895-7
Printed in Great Britain by
Arthur H. Stockwell Ltd
Torrs Park   Ilfracombe
Devon

Contents

A Day of Peace

The day was one of peace and tranquillity:
There were no raised voices
And, though I was alone,
There was a beauty about the day.

Though it was winter,
And rather a cold chill was in the air,
I could do today what I desired
With no one to disturb me with idle chatter
Or children saying, "I'm bored – what can I do now?"
I could enjoy the day in a quiet way
With just my little cat for company.

A Hope for Christmas

Christmas is here again.
For some it brings the joy of a family reunion;
For others it brings the pain of finding themselves on their own
Without family or friends around them.
When happiness abounds
In many homes throughout the land,
There are many sad young people who are homeless and alone,
And the only kindness comes
From the Salvation Army or YMCA on Christmas Day.
When other people are so happy and so glad,
We should help them where we can –
These people who are in need of our love and care –
And hope that the New Year will bring joy, peace and love.

A Lovely Day in April

The sun is shining brightly,
This early day in spring.
I wonder what awakening
To me this spring will bring.

Will this year bring discoveries?
Will it be a year of joys?
A time for new beginnings,
Of new things to enjoy?

We can only hope tomorrow
We'll see the sun's bright rays,
When life will have new meaning
And bring us joyful days.

The New Beginning

The day of new beginnings,
When everything is new –
A time when loved ones will be there,
And hours will be happy too.

The whole of life's a journey –
And it's lonely on your own –
A time for meeting friends together,
A time to grow.

We must make the most of each day,
For time is very short;
And happiness is there for us
If we will only look into our hearts.

A Special Son

A son doesn't need to be tall, dark or handsome to be dear to me,
Though he is handsome and attractive in his way.
He may not be rich or famous or a power in the world,
But what he has you can never take away.
Though he's often cheeky, I know he has a kind heart
For he's there when others have moved away;
He's there when people need him,
When no one else is around
For they have no time to spare, they say.
He's kind and caring to the people that he meets;
And when he's needed they know he'll be there.
To have a son like this is fortunate indeed,
For one like him is rare.

A Sunny Day in Winter

It's a lovely day in winter. The sun is shining brightly –
It's as if spring is in the air
As I walk down the street with my little cat today,
For she is frightened to go out on her own.

There are dangers all around for her to see –
A woman vacuuming her car makes a strange sound,
And dogs on leads are things to avoid.

Cars go by as they travel down the road –
Chloe sits on the wall and watches the world pass by
(A thing she never tires of). It's all new to her eyes –
It's a world of wonder and surprise each day.

She's like a child seeing the world for the first time –
It's fresh and interesting and fascinatingly new.
And she is happy that I'm with her too.
She comes to me to stroke her coat,
Then we continue on our way,
Then return home together to go out another day.

A True Friend

A friend who is there for you is one who is true;
One who walks away when trouble brews
Is not a friend for you.
A friend is like a rare gem – a diamond or a pearl –
And should be treasured,
For few who come into your life
Will care to be a sister or a brother.

People have their own concerns, their own dreams to realise,
And have little time for others with their sorrows and their joys.
When you have such a friend it puts a glow around your heart
And the world seems a better place,
With gladness all about.

Friendship is a love that asks for nothing in return,
And it is a priceless treasure for which we all yearn.

A Young Girl's Dream

The years have passed away. Was it just a dream?
Did it really happen? Was it yesterday?
Was it really me?

We were so happy whilst it lasted;
They were such perfect days.
I thought it would last for ever.
If only you had stayed!

And though we have parted,
Through no fault of our own,
Part of my heart went with you –
It was always yours to own.

They thought I was not serious
Because I was young;
That it would last a short time
And I would have some fun.

Though many years have passed,
It feels like yesterday;
And if tomorrow we would be together,
It would seem as if you'd never been away.

The Accidental Family

Your family will be there for you
For, whatever they may say, they all love you.
People say things in haste,
Though in their hearts
You will always have a place.

It's love that holds a family together
Through any trouble you can weather,
For love is the strongest bond, and lasts
Even when life is past.

Your family will be there for you
And so will friends who are true.
A new baby brings with it love –
It's the most wonderful thing
And makes the heart sing
And binds the family together with love.

Christmas Joys

Christmas fills people's hearts with joy –
Though for some not because of the birth of a boy,
But for the reunion of families far and near
And of friends that we hold most dear.

This is the time to spread love around,
When our hearts are glad and joy abounds,
For love is the only thing that counts –
Not material gain or pound notes.
For love is there for all to see in the love we have for our family.

Christmas Memories

On Christmas Day I was on my own
With just my cat for company.
When I'm alone she stays with me
As if she thinks she must look after me.

It wasn't a sad day, for I spend most of my days alone.
Nor was I lonely, and there were no raised voices,
No one to complain he was bored.
The house was quiet with a peaceful serenity
And a feeling of heavenly love around me.

One can feel lonely in a room full of people
If there is no bond of friendship,
Affection or mutual interest.
You still feel on your own if you have no one to belong to or care
Or ask you around for a coffee, or pass the time of day;
But there are those without a home,
And no one cares if they live or die.

It is them we must care about, not you or I
Who live in our cosy homes and watch the world pass by.

Dearest Love

One day we will be together in that land above the skies;
Then no one will again part us, as love like ours never dies.
We will be as we were when young.
Oh, my darling, how I wish we could have been together,
And spent our lives as one!

Do not remember the sad days, darling,
Only the things that made you smile –
The happiness that was around us.
I was only with you a short while,
But I remember those days clearly.

Even though you were little more than a child
You had a maturity beyond your years
And I saw the love that was in your eyes.
I am sorry I filled your eyes with tears, dear,
When you had stars in your eyes.
The memories of those moments have stayed with me, dearest;
The love I had for you never dies.

Emily Sarah

Emily Sarah will soon be free,
Able to be what she wants to be.
Emily Sarah has the world at her feet;
Many famous people she will meet.
Emily Sarah's life will be happy and free,
For she will be able to live as she wants to be
Without anyone telling her what she must do.
For with education your life is for you.
Emily Sarah, I wish you much joy
For life will be there for you to enjoy.
Emily Sarah, the day will soon be here
When all of the people will stand up and cheer.

Every Ending Is a New Beginning

Every ending is a new beginning,
A hope for things to come.
We can only hope tomorrow
Will bring the things for which we long.

Every ending is a new beginning,
A promise of things reborn,
A new day far more happy
Than the life that we have known.

Every ending is a new beginning,
With a hope of friendship true,
Of love that's never-ending,
And happy days with you.

Farewell My Love, Farewell

Farewell my love, farewell –
The saddest words that fell
From any young man's lips, to some young girl.
For what he meant was goodbye,
Which caused the girl to cry
And feel rejected by the man she loved.
The pain was so intense – she thought herself worthless
For the man she loved could cause her distress like this,
When she had loved him so.
What was it about her he disliked,
That he could cause her pain like this, and let her go,
And leave her alone, and on her own,
Not caring if she lived or died?
She was just his plaything,
His toy to discard as if he was still a child.

Love Was in the Air

Love was in the air, and we didn't have a care.
We saw beauty everywhere,
And our happiness to share.

Love transforms us all;
And we didn't need to call and say, "I love you,"
For love was there for all to see in the happiness of you and me.
And our dreams and schemes of our future too.

Oh, how I love you! –
I heard it in the birds' song too
For love was in the air.

Freedom

Today is a special day for me.
It is the first day that I am free
Of all the cares that tied me down.

I do not need to frown, or sigh or look up to the sky
For I am free –
Free to make my way in the world
Not beholden to anyone but me;
To lead my life in any way I choose;
For I have nothing more to lose.

My work is done for my family –
They have moved far away.
I must make a life of my own
And I must be happy just to be me.

Girls You Shouldn't Marry

Don't marry a girl with a career,
If companionship is what you seek.
Your marriage will be by text and phone –
You'll only see her once a week.

Don't marry a girl who owns a horse,
No matter how much grace she's blessed.
The stables will be her first home –
You'll always come out second best.

Don't marry a girl who knows her mind,
If it's the pants you want to wear.
She'll outsmart you at every turn –
You're just a man, you've not a prayer.

For these girls will not cook your meals,
And none will iron your shirts.
If that's what you want from a marriage,
Be careful with whom you flirt.

Home

As I walked down the road,
I passed the house I had lived in for twenty-five years.
The happiness and pain that I had known there
Could not be described in any words.
I felt a sadness when I passed
The house where I had spent so many years,
The house I had entered as a young bride.
Oh, those long-past years!

I thought of all my hopes and dreams,
The laughter and the tears:
Some things turned out better than I had hoped,
Others filled me with fears.

The most blessed place is home,
However far away we may roam.
There is no place more lovely,
However lowly it may seem to strangers,
However shabby and worn,
For love shines out of the doors and windows.
For that's where happiness is complete
And can be found in any street.

Life's Success

What is of importance? What do I want?
It isn't riches, it isn't success; it's just health and happiness.
How can I find it? Where will I search?
By looking into your heart you'll discover your worth.

Life is so precious, the days are so short –
It's love that matters, not what you've bought.
Though we need money for our day-to-day needs
Money alone will not fulfil all our dreams.

It's freedom of thought, and friends that are true
And a loving family surrounding you.
If you have these things you are rich indeed,
Then you have everything you may need,
But all the money in the world won't give these things to you.
When you live alone in your beautiful house
With its wonderful view
These things are nothing without love in your heart.

That's what life is about: having people who care –
The ones you can share with, who'll always be there.
Then you are rich; without it you're poor.
With love in your heart you can't ask for more.

Love Is the Greatest Thing

Love is the greatest thing in heaven and earth.
Without it, life has no worth,
There is no meaning, there is no mirth,
For love alone gives life rebirth.

People will grow in mind and soul
Only when they love behold.
Without it life is an empty shell.
We can only hope that our lives will tell us all is well.

We can find love as well as friendship,
And only then will life give us happiness –
When love is around for all to see
In the blessings bestowed on you and me.

Love's Gift

The most precious gift is love;
It comes from Heaven above.
It costs nothing, but it is more precious than any gem.
It removes all pain and puts joy into the heart.

The world seems a more beautiful place.
Many men have loved for the beauty of a face –
This is a fleeting thing, and may not be one of grace –
Instead of looking for qualities of kindness,
Compassion and generosity of mind.
Only in this way true love you will find.

Mother's Last Words

Now that I am gone away
I hope that you will sometimes smile
When you think of me,
Though I shall still be around.

I who have loved you long
Will be there to help and guide you.
If you will listen to your heart
You will surely hear me.

No one ever dies,
We just go to a new dimension in the skies.
Look at the stars.
I'll be there looking on the world so fair,
Hoping that you are aware
Of the wonders God has put there for all to see.
And, perhaps, think of me.

My Friend Across the Sea

I have a dear friend whom I never see,
Who lives three thousand miles from me.
But it is as if he lives next door.
Words of kindness he does pour,
In letters and emails, to
'A friend who really cares for you'.

I knew him when he was a child,
When he lived here quite close to me.
Now that he lives so far away,
I hear by email every day.
It's as if he's at my side.
He puts gladness in my heart and mind,
For when you're old there are few who care –
A person like this is very rare.

My Husband

I remember your smile when you looked at me,
The way you walked beside me and held my hand.
I was always glad when you were near
And I had nothing more to fear.

And now you no longer on this earth reside,
I think of you and still feel glad
Of the precious years we spent together,
Which gave us happiness without measure.
I now sit here and shed a tear for that happy yesteryear.

Life's Dreams

The love you have for others will soon return to you,
For now the dreams you've had are coming into view.

Your life's tapestry is nearly woven, and you will see your destiny;
All will be well, for love is all around for you to see.

You will only have to wait a little longer
For all to be revealed.
Life seems like a dream, but sometimes dreams come true,
And that's what I wish for you.

Spring Is Nearly Here

Spring is nearly here,
Though the weather may be cold and shivery,
With snowstorms followed by rain.

The days can be dark and dreary,
When you do not want to go out but sit at home,
When days are short and nights are long.

But winter will soon be gone,
And nature will once again renew itself
With baby animals, plants and trees.

The world will be wonderful and new,
And spring will be with us again, for all to view.

Summer Days

Summer is the part of the year,
With its searing heat, which I can only meet with tiredness.
I feel that I'm slowly moving through a haze
And wish for cooler days and winds that blow.

It's so rare to have this weather,
So I should not complain
But remember the snow and sleeted rain.
This will be with us soon once more again
In our cold winter weather.

The Happy Man

To be happy, a man must find a good wife –
One with whom he would wish to share all of his life.
To find her may be a difficult task.

Some find a girl, but it doesn't last.
He might find her living next door,
Or he may find he has the world to scour.

When he finds her he should not let her go,
For he may not find another he could so love and adore.

It is difficult to find a girl who would be his ideal bride,
Whom he would wish to keep all his life at his side.
Happy is a man who finds a girl such as this,
As all of his life he will live in bliss.

The Beauty of Scotland

Scotland is a place so fair,
With mountains, rivers and majestic trees
Gently swaying in the breeze.
The beauty is quite awesome, and you feel God's presence too
In the peace and tranquillity that is to be found in the view.

Many people look for beauty in paintings and works of art,
In fine buildings and houses, instead of looking into their hearts
And seeing all the beauty which is around all the time.
This is God's gift to us and makes our world sublime.

The Child

Today I am but a child,
But tomorrow, soon, I will be a woman.
This will bring me different hopes, dreams and wishes,
Some of which are unknown to me as yet
And others only half-thought ideas still forming in my mind.

I must learn to love, accept people as they are
With their flaws, kindness and good deeds,
Not expecting perfection in all things
And realising that other people have their own hopes and dreams
And they are just as important as mine are to me.

Our ways are different, for we must follow our own paths
We should show kindness, compassion,
Concern and consideration for others,
As we travel through our life,
Not thinking that only our wishes matter.
All people are important in their own diverse ways,
And there is cleverness of many different kinds.

Those who stand in the background may have the most insight.
With age comes knowledge, wisdom,
And knowing what is right.
The whole of life is a school
Where we must learn our lessons every day
To improve our character, our disposition,
Our outlook on the world;
And our hope should be that we might leave
This world a better place
For our just being here.
For the best thing we can leave behind
Is our good name, and not our fame.

The Dawning of a New Era

The day was one of discovery – a day when all was new.
It was one of satisfaction,
For all my troubles they were through.
As I looked upon the new day, without feeling of regret,
I felt a new era was dawning. I had no need to be upset.

For life suddenly had a new meaning
With the birth of a new child.
A new life was beginning,
With all the excitement that gave me pride.
We can't foretell the future, and know what it will bring.

But with the joy of a new life coming to this earth
We can believe that tomorrow
Will bring joy and love something of real worth.

The Family

Home is where the family is.
If only people would realise this!
It isn't in a far-off country,
Thinking you are free,
Doing what you want to be.

Any place can be your home
If from your family you do not roam.
But when they are far away
It's just the same from day to day.
Your heart aches, for they aren't there.

It just seems that they do not care,
For if they did they would not have ventured far away
And you could have seen them, if you wished, each day.
They left you sad with tears in your eyes
For the love you had for them they did not prize.

The Glories of Nature

I gazed up at the sky
Watching the birds fly by,
For all the world to see
Like a picture painted by a great master
Of wonder and majesty.

How glorious is nature with her many differing scenes,
Ever-changing, never-tiring, fulfilling many dreams!
Its beauty and loveliness, its changing seasons
Bring joy to us without us having any reasons.

The Golden Day

It was a day of rare beauty,
A day when everything was fair,
A time for solitude, to gaze at loveliness around you there.
The earth is a place of wonder and delight
That fills us with awe at the majesty and artistry
Of the hills, trees, and mountain streams
In the ever-changing view that is for ever new.

The Happy Day

The day was just like any other.
Nothing happened, no one called;
Only my friend Janette phoned,
And I was outside at the dustbin when she telephoned.
However, the day was peaceful and the weather kept fine
And I was feeling better than I had for some considerable time.

So, all in all, it was a good day,
And the signs were that spring was on the way,
And my cat Chloe and I went out for a little walk that day.
This amused the neighbours as they saw us both pass by
As I strolled along the street,
Whilst she walked around the gardens kept so neat.

My cat looked at the plants and examined them with care,
Just as if she was the gardener, to see if she had work there.
Happiness can be found in such small mundane things as these.
See the world through your cat's eyes,
And note the merriment it brings.

The Happy Journey

The day was one of excitement when everything was new,
Full of new possibilities,
And love that was wonderful and true.
We each have to have our dreams,
For them to change our life,
And be a new awakening –
The promise that life can have a bright new meaning,
A wonderful new hue.

It's a time for new beginnings, a time for happiness to grow,
When anything is possible.
You will feel a glow as if a light had been turned on,
As if a new era had begun –
As if all our troubles of yesterday were over
And happiness was here for everyone.

Though we tread our different paths in life,
Sometimes we meet along the way,
And spend a little time with,
Someone who has something new to say.
Then life has a new meaning,
Even a glimpse of what's to come,
But life is a lonely journey when you travel on your own.

There are those who love us, and those who really care,
Though perhaps they do not show it, except by being there.

I hope the day will come when life will be happy for all to see,
With a united family with love and harmony.

The Holiday

Today was a holiday.
I went to my church today.
It should have been a day of rejoicing,
But I was on my own.

My husband has long gone to spirit,
And my children all have flown.
The house was peaceful and serene
With just my little cat for company.

There was no need to be sad,
For I was not alone
With the peace and tranquillity –
God spent the day with me.

The Isle of Wight

On Thursday I'm going away on my holiday
Across the sea to an island peaceful and serene –
A place of beauty and tranquillity,
Where I can forget the big city.

I forget my cares and think of nothing but the joy of being there.
I refresh myself on an island fair.
It seems it's so far away, yet lies so close to England's shores
And though it's separated by the sea
It seems as if it were a thousand miles to you and me.

The island called the Isle of Wight
Is a joy to see –
A place of loveliness, with its old-time beauty.

The Magnolia Tree

Spring was in the air today.
As I walked down the street
I saw a wondrous sight
In the beauty of a magnolia tree –
A thing of rare beauty.

I stood and gazed at it with awe.
A finer sight you could not see
Than the flowers of the magnolia tree.
I see God's artistry in the glory of this tree.

It is sad when people are so busy
Going to and fro to work and play
That they neglect to see the splendour
That's around them every day.

Because it's free to see, for you and me,
They do not notice or even care.
But this is the greatest art of all,
Which God has created for all to see
In the creation of the magnolia tree.

The Meaning of Love

'I love you' is but three little words,
And such a simple thing to say.
They are the sweetest words that are ever heard,
And yet they're uttered every day.

For love is not I, but we,
And we have to work together to live in harmony.
Love is wonderful when two hearts beat as one.

When two people have a single aim in life,
A common goal to reach,
Their lives will be as one, and will be complete.

Without love, life would be a disaster,
And nothing could cure it, you couldn't stick on a plaster.
Only love can heal it,
And only love can make life worthwhile.

Your heart will tell you when you're going wrong,
And not until you're together can you sing your own love song.

The Mother

I am an old woman, but what does that mean?
Though life's mostly memories, I still have my dreams –
Things longed for tomorrow, and hoped for today.
There are many adventures and games still to play.

Though we are old, we still have our joys,
Our plans for the future for our girls and our boys.
And we hope that the New Year will fulfil all our dreams,
We will see a bright future and success to our schemes.

Whilst there is life, there hope reigns supreme –
Anything is possible if you hold on to that dream.
Though the years say you're old, in your heart you are young
So anything is possible – remember that, son.

The New Direction

Your life is now taking a new direction,
All your hopes and dreams will be realised,
Soon you will have friends who really care about you
And a love that never ends or dies.

If we only live in the past, we cannot see the clear blue skies
Only the sad yesterdays, and the tears that filled your eyes.
Life on your own is a lonely path to follow,
A hard road for your feet to tread;
But, with friends around to help you,
You can walk with a firm and trusting step,
For there are those around us we can trust.
This makes the world a wonderful place for both of us.

The New Year

The New Year is here again.
What will the New Year bring?
Will it bring happiness and success
And joy in everything?

We cannot foretell the future;
We can only walk our path with hope,
And hope that the year will be one of note.

We must look to the future
With the promise of better things to come
And the joy and fulfilment of life
With love around for everyone.

What is the Price of Peace

When will there be peace in the world?
Is it just a dream?
When will it be a reality?
Will it ever be seen?

First we have to live in peace with our families,
Care for our neighbours and friends –
Not just for people we see each day,
But people from other lands.

Only when we spread love and kindness around
In other nations and far-off countries,
Will peace come into our lives.
When love is for others, not just for ourselves,
Then peace will abide in the land
And be a fit place for man to dwell.

The Predator

Death is all around us, with great big pointy teeth.
It is a pussy cat, with a face which is very sweet,
Who purrs and rubs around your legs, and sits upon your knee,
And kisses you all over, and loves you tenderly.

When she's in the garden there's another side to see:
She'll take baby birds from their nests,
And bring them home to me;
And live mice I've rescued and put them under a tree;
There was even a pigeon (a very large one, I did see),
Which she brought in through the cat flap as a present for me.

The other day I heard the plaintive cry of a bird,
And went to investigate the sound I had heard.
All there was left to see was just one feather –
Everything else had been eaten by Chloe for her tea.

I saw her lick her lips; she
Looked at me with eyes of sweet innocence.
She seemed to say to me,
"I haven't been naughty. I'm a good girl.
Why are you so cross with me?"

The Price of Peace

The price of peace –
Peace at what price?
You have to have a voice
Or people will destroy you –
You don't have a choice.

You must speak out,
Or you won't last.
You must remember what happened in the past
When they caused you pain,
And put you to shame.
You must hold your head high,
And look them in the eye,
And hold on to your good name,
And hope they will see the real person that is me,
And turn away from the evil.

The Special Child

The New Year brings new beginnings:
A hope for better things to come –
A year of peace and happiness, a year of great blessings.
Children's voices ring out and sing –
A year when a special child is born and the happiness it brings.

Who'll spread joy around, with goodwill, and love profound,
And all the bells will ring
For it's the beginning of a new era.
So clap your hands and sing,
For God's love is around us and the angels all will sing.

The Strange Woman

There's this strange woman – sometimes she stops and stares.
There are days she talks a lot;
Other times it's as if she isn't there.
There are times she's friendly; others when she's aloof.
What's the matter with this woman? Aren't we good enough?

She tries to help people that she meets along the way.
Some people are grateful; others wish she'd go away.
She looks ordinary enough,
There's nothing unusual in her demeanour,
So why are they put off? What's the matter with her?

She has a secret illness and people aren't aware.
Some just lack compassion, or simply do not care.
It's a mental illness – not an obvious affliction –
And she isn't understood with her invisible condition.

The Strong Man

It is said to err is human and to forgive divine,
When God made man a little lower than the angels
So they should spiritually aspire to climb.

No man living is without sin,
Or he would not on this earth reside,
For earth is just a school where his lessons must be learnt
For the benefit of mankind.
If his life were easy, it would not make him strong;
It's the difficulties he meets as he journeys on
That will improve his character as he travels life's road,
For steel has to be tempered by fire to be strong, we are told.

Though his life won't be easy, he'll meet the challenges of life –
Whether they mean happiness or whether they mean strife.
A weak man will be broken by his trials of life;
A strong man will bend a little, but grow strong and upright.
He will succeed in all he aspires to do,
And so he is a man to be respected and admired
And to be looked up to.

The Wonder of Spring

Spring will be here again to bring us cheer
From cold, icy, wet days of winter
With hail and snow, and winter blasts of wind
Blowing us down the streets
As we go about our daily tasks.

Whatever the weather may bring,
We have to carry on with the flow of things;
But each new day brings us nearer to those warm, sunny days
When the daffodils and bluebells grow,
And trees, with their blossoms all around in a mass of wonder
And a delight for all to see
As if it was just meant for me –
The wonders which spring shows to me.

The Wonderful Day

It was a day when the sun was shining,
A day when spring was in the air,
A day of new beginnings when you didn't have a care.

The world seemed fresh and new
And seemed to burst out from the heart,
Bringing happiness to you.

Love is the greatest gift. It lifts the heart
And makes us want to sing and dance
And hear the joyful bells ring out clear.

Life has a new beginning, a special new meaning,
For the earth is renewed again
And has awoken from its dreaming.

Time Goes By

As time goes by, it seems but yesterday
When we were young, so full of hope for the years to come.

Where have all these years gone?
They've passed by in just the twinkling of an eye.

I am now in the autumn of my days.
I feel that I may at last come into my own
And smile as I am now my own person,
The person I had hoped to be.

But perhaps it is now too late for me –
Maybe my work is done
And it's just now time to sit in the sun.

I hope that is not so, for I still have my dreams
Of a wonderful tomorrow of happiness instead of sorrow.

Time Passes So Quickly

Time passes so quickly, as if it's been a dream.
Only look into your heart – it's as if it's never been.
Did it really happen? Were you really there?
How many days were happiness; how many were despair?

It's only when you look into the mirror
That you see the passage of time.
Where has that young girl gone?
What happened to her smile?
We should only count the years with the blessings all around
And the love of all the people that our life surrounds.

True Love

When a young man says "I love you"
What does it really mean?
I like your pretty face, your smile,
Your youthful figure, your grace
And that you are serene.

How will he feel when she is no longer young, or so pretty?
Will he change her for a younger one?
Or will he say, "I love her for her kindness and concern –
The help she gives to others without thought of return.
Never mind if she is less pleasing to the eye,
She is my treasure and the apple of my eye."

Uncertainty

We do not know what the future holds;
We only know, as our life unfolds,
That we must follow the path, and journey on,
And carry the load which life has given us.

We must be bold to do what's right, even if it means
We have to fight for our convictions, our beliefs.
There are those who would only cause us grief,
But we should live with mercy, justice and peace,
Which is the way to make our life complete.

What Is the Future?

My daughter, what will her future be?
Will she succeed without her freedom to do what she feels?
Or will she realise that 'life isn't just for me',
But considering others as well as her dreams?

Life never turns out as we had planned –
Sometimes it's better; other times sad.
There are always surprises as we travel life's road.
We can even be glad that our life has taken a different direction,
An unexpected turn – that's how life goes.

For a happy and successful marriage to last
We have to make sacrifices and not live in the past.
Nothing worthwhile is easy,
Or lasts without effort, love and trust.
We can only hope that love will be enough
To bring about the things that make life worthwhile,
So that we should feel we want to sing, dance and smile;
So the future will be better, with a brighter glow;
So we should have more understanding and happiness
Within us for all to know.

When You Are Old

When you are old no one cares about you.
The days seem long and never-ending.
You look for meaning in your life,
A purpose to follow,
To forget your trouble and your sorrow.

The days go by but are not of any consequence.
You hope tomorrow will bring you joy, not grief,
With children's laughter,
And dreams of life filled with joy, not strife.
A world of happiness instead of loneliness,
Where people speak and hold out their hands of friendship,
Where people are happy and life is sweet.

Few people have time to talk to you –
Their lives are busy, they have schedules to keep.

You feel the world is whizzing by you,
But it's almost as if you were asleep
And waiting for the prince to wake you with a kiss,
And break the spell
And make your life complete.